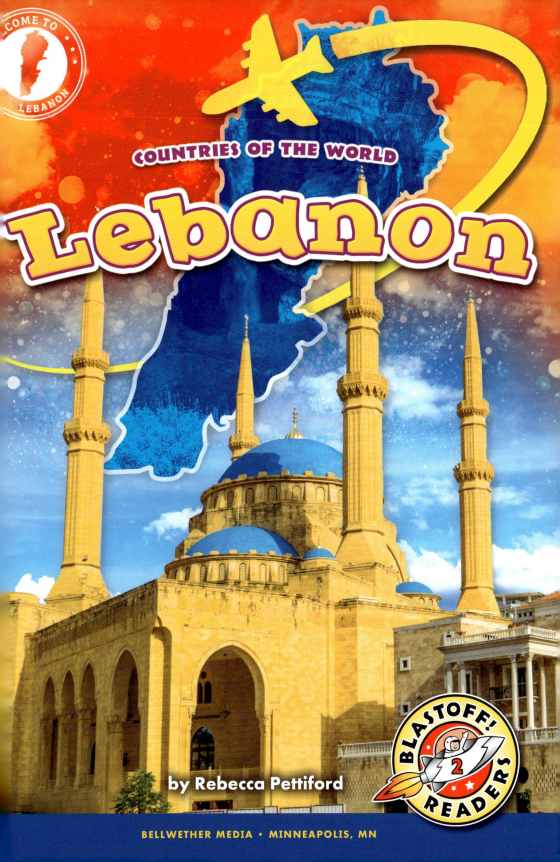

**Blastoff! Readers** are carefully developed by literacy experts to build reading stamina and move students toward fluency by combining standards-based content with developmentally appropriate text.

 **Level 1** provides the most support through repetition of high-frequency words, light text, predictable sentence patterns, and strong visual support.

 **Level 2** offers early readers a bit more challenge through varied sentences, increased text load, and text-supportive special features.

 **Level 3** advances early-fluent readers toward fluency through increased text load, less reliance on photos, advancing concepts, longer sentences, and more complex special features.

★ **Blastoff! Universe**

Reading Level — Grade K — Grades 1–3 — Grade 4

This edition first published in 2026 by Bellwether Media, Inc.

No part of this publication may be reproduced in whole or in part without written permission of the publisher. For information regarding permission, write to Bellwether Media, Inc., Attention: Permissions Department, 3500 American Blvd W, Suite 150, Bloomington, MN 55431.

Library of Congress Cataloging-in-Publication Data

LC record for Lebanon available at: https://lccn.loc.gov/2025015026

Text copyright © 2026 by Bellwether Media, Inc. BLASTOFF! READERS and associated logos are trademarks and/or registered trademarks of Bellwether Media, Inc. Bellwether Media is a division of FlutterBee Education Group.

Editor: Betsy Rathburn   Designer: Laura Sowers

Printed in the United States of America, North Mankato, MN.

# Table of Contents

All About Lebanon        4
Land and Animals         6
Life in Lebanon         12
Lebanon Facts           20
Glossary                22
To Learn More           23
Index                   24

# All About Lebanon

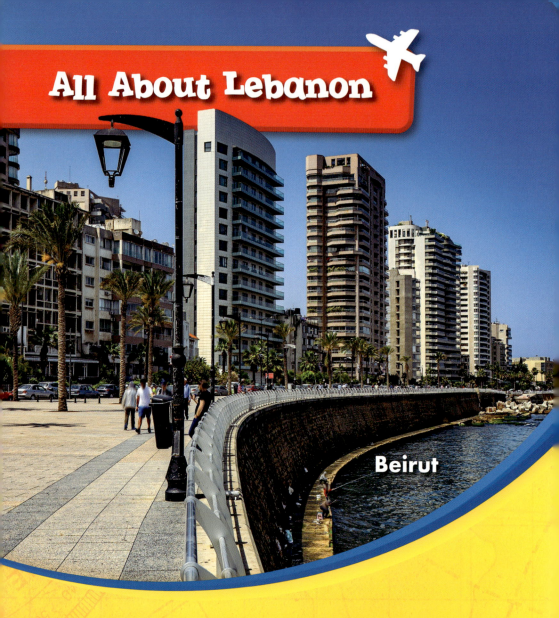

Beirut

Lebanon is a small country in the **Middle East**. It borders the Mediterranean Sea. The capital is Beirut.

Lebanon is known for its cedar trees and delicious food.

# Land and Animals

Mountains cover most of the country. Cedar trees grow in the northern mountains.

Valleys lie between the mountains. Sandy beaches line the **coastal plain**.

cedar tree

## Qurnat al-Sawdā'

**Size:** 10,131 feet (3,088 meters) tall
**Famous For:** Lebanon's highest peak

Winters in Lebanon are cool. Most rain falls between October and April. The high mountain peaks get a lot of snow.

Summers are hot and dry.

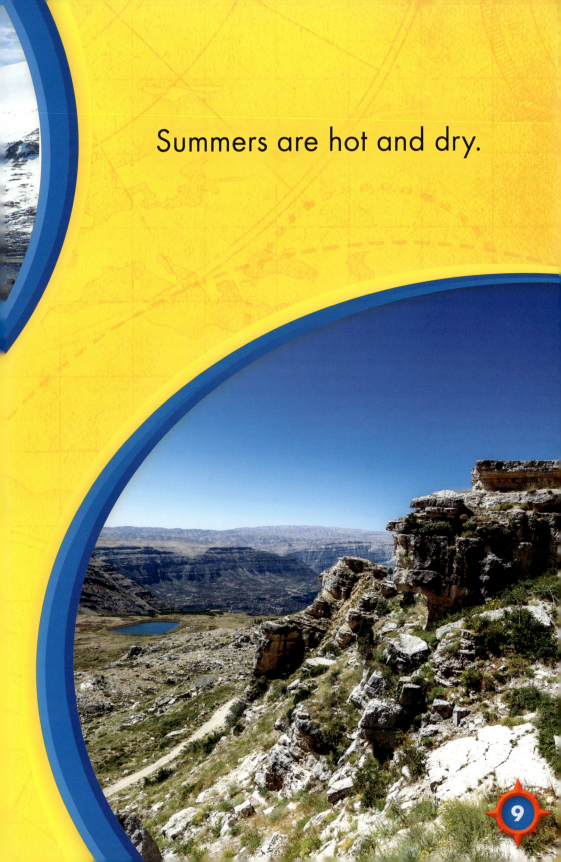

Golden jackals roam the valleys. Finches make nests in mountain rocks.

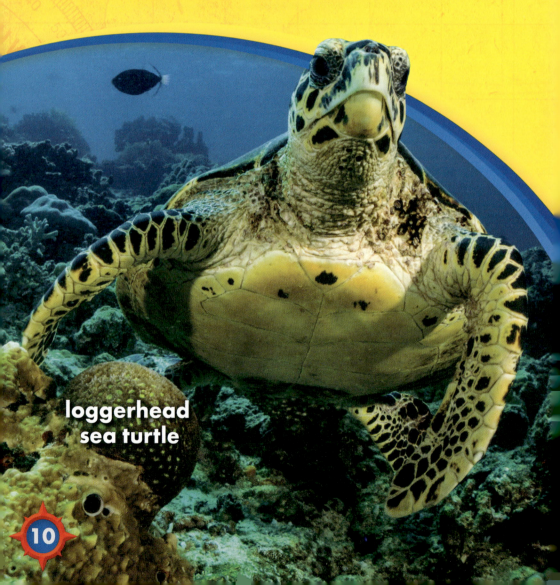

loggerhead sea turtle

Sea turtles swim in the Mediterranean. Striped hyenas hunt almost everywhere!

# Life in Lebanon

Most Lebanese people are **Arab**. They speak Arabic. Some people speak French and English.

Over half of the people are **Muslims**. About one in three people are **Christians**.

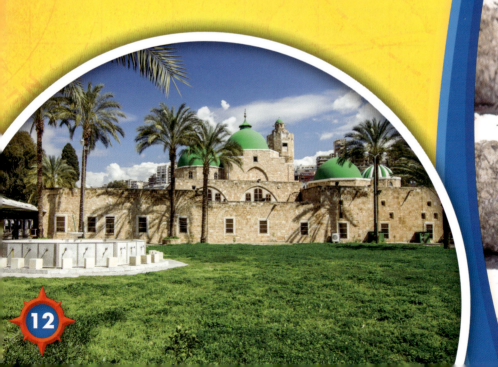

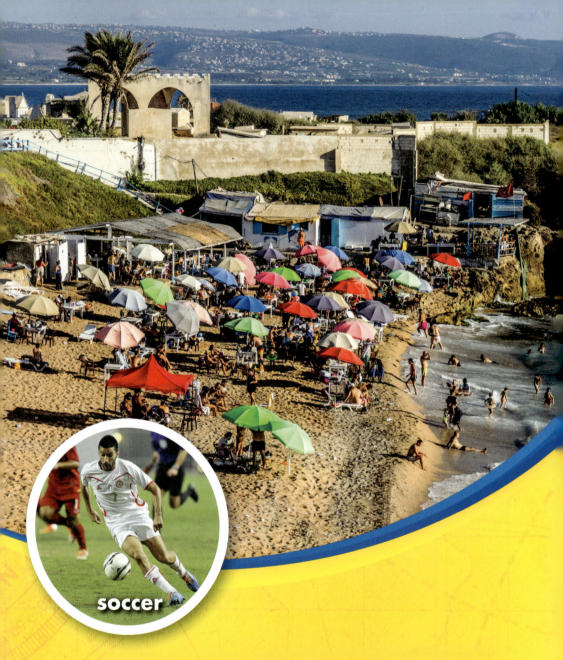

soccer

Many people play basketball and soccer. Others like to hike and go to beaches.

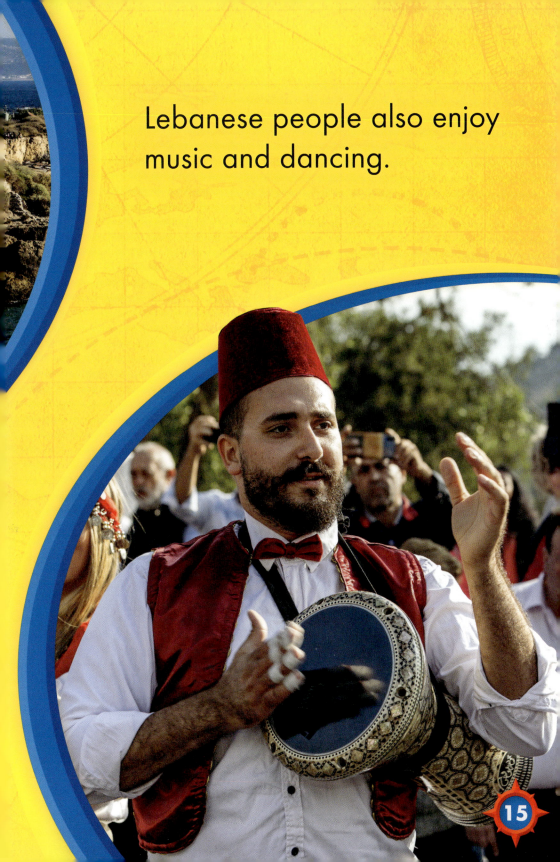

Lebanese people also enjoy music and dancing.

*Kibbeh* is a meat and **bulgur** dish. Hummus is a popular dip for vegetables and bread.

### Lebanese Foods

kibbeh

hummus

tabbouleh

katayef

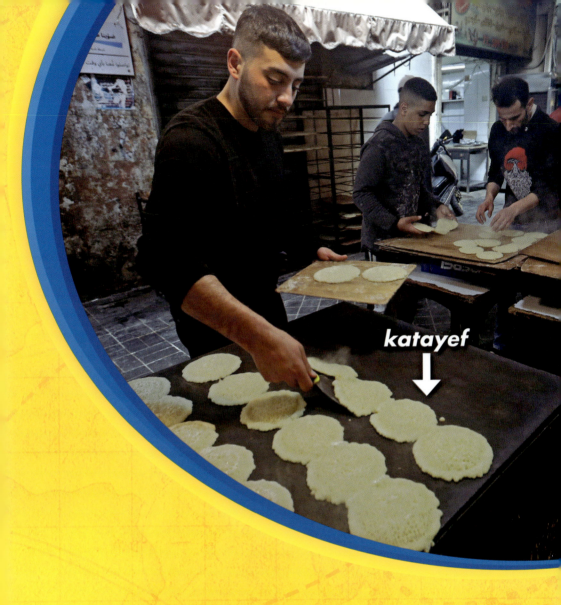

Tabbouleh is a bulgur salad.
*Katayef* are sweet, folded pancakes.

In February and March, people go to Al Bustan. It is a music and arts **festival**.

*Eid al-Fitr* marks the end of Ramadan. People **celebrate** with family!

*Eid al-Fitr*

# Lebanon Facts

**Size:**
4,015 square miles
(10,400 square kilometers)

**Population:**
5,364,482 (2024)

**National Holiday:**
Independence Day (November 22)

**Main Language:**
Arabic

**Capital City:**
Beirut

## Famous Face

**Name:** Fairuz

**Famous For:** singer and actress

# Religions

Christian: 32%

other: 1%

Muslim: 67%

# Top Landmarks

**Cedars of God**

**Mohammad al-Amin Mosque**

**National Museum of Beirut**

# Glossary

**Arab**—related to people who live mostly in the Middle East and northern Africa

**bulgur**—related to a whole grain made from cracked wheat

**celebrate**—to do something special or fun for an event, occasion, or holiday

**Christians**—people who believe in the words of Jesus Christ

**coastal plain**—an area of flat land with few trees that lies next to the ocean

**festival**—a time or event of celebration

**Middle East**—a region of southwestern Asia and northern Africa; the Middle East includes Egypt, Lebanon, Iran, Iraq, Israel, Saudi Arabia, Syria, and other nearby countries.

**Muslims**—people of the Islamic faith; Muslims follow the teachings of Muhammad as told to him from Allah.

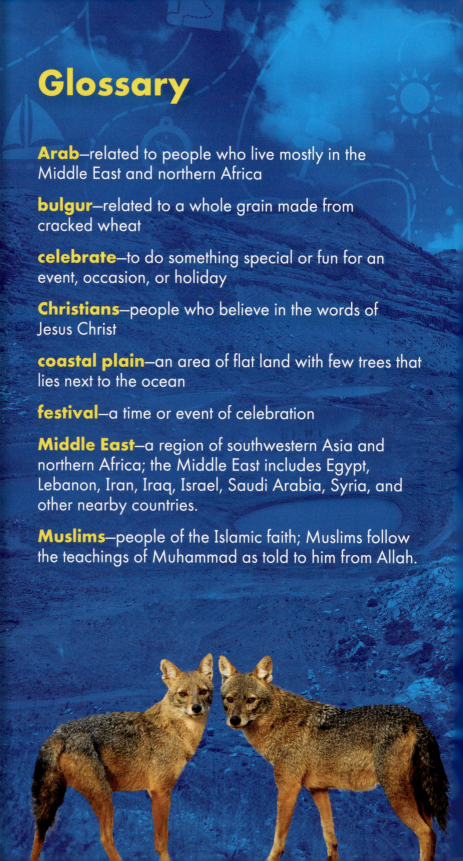

# To Learn More

### AT THE LIBRARY

Barnes, Rachael. *Israel*. Minneapolis, Minn.: Bellwether Media, 2023.

Golkar, Golriz. *Islamic Festivals and Traditions*. North Mankato, Minn.: Pebble, 2025.

Leaf, Christina. *Arabic*. Minneapolis, Minn.: Bellwether Media, 2026.

### ON THE WEB

# FACTSURFER

Factsurfer.com gives you a safe, fun way to find more information.

1. Go to www.factsurfer.com.

2. Enter "Lebanon" into the search box and click 🔍.

3. Select your book cover to see a list of related content.

# Index

Al Bustan, 18, 19
animals, 10, 11
Arabic, 12, 13
basketball, 14
beaches, 6, 14
Beirut, 4, 5
capital (see Beirut)
cedar trees, 5, 6
Christians, 12
coastal plain, 6
dancing, 15
*Eid al-Fitr*, 18
English, 12
food, 5, 16, 17
French, 12
hike, 14
Lebanon facts, 20–21
map, 5
Mediterranean Sea, 4, 11
Middle East, 4
mountains, 6, 7, 8, 10

music, 15, 18
Muslims, 12
people, 12, 14, 15, 18
Qurnat al-Sawdā', 7
rain, 8
say hello, 13
snow, 8
soccer, 14
summers, 9
valleys, 6, 10
winters, 8

The images in this book are reproduced through the courtesy of: Stock Photos 2000, front cover, p. 21 (National Museum of Beirut); CWresh, p. 3; WitR, pp. 4-5; Sybille Yates, p. 6; David Dennis, pp. 6-7; JSK/ Alamy Stock Photo, pp. 8-9; paul saad, pp. 9, 15, 21 (Mohammad al-Amin Mosque); Subphoto, pp. 10-11; Juan Carlos Munoz, p. 11 (golden jackal); AGAMI Photo Agency/ Alamy Stock Photo, p. 11 (crimson-winged finch); Miroslav Halama, p. 11 (loggerhead sea turtle); Andrew M. Allport, p. 11 (striped hyena); savas_bozkaya, p. 12; Greg Balfour Evans/ Alamy Stock Photo, pp. 12-13; Rnoid, p. 14 (soccer); Matyas Rehak, pp. 14-15; muhammed yasin irik, p. 16 (*kibbeh*); Natalia Klenova, p. 16 (hummus); Svetlana Monyakova, p. 16 (tabbouleh); Veliavik, p. 16 (*katayef*); MAHMOUD ZAYYAT/ Getty Images, p. 17; Pressmaster, p. 18; Sipa USA/ Alamy Stock Photo, pp. 18-19; Umair Zia Khan, p. 20 (flag); Francois LOCHON/ Getty Images, p. 20 (Fairuz); henry melki, p. 21 (Cedars of God); Martin Mecnarowski, p. 22.